A Hard Row to Hoe: The Story That Almost Wasn't Told

By C. M. Hindman

To my loving wife, family and friends. Thank you for all of

your love and support.

A special thanks to my wonderful wife for assisting with

this book.

Introduction

It was a hard life, a tough life. I had a rough start, but I made it. And by God's grace, I made a good life. These are the stories of my life, in my own words. Maybe you can relate to some of them. Maybe you'll be surprised by some of them. Maybe you will be touched by one or two. Join me as I share my stories, and I hope you enjoy the journey.

My Family

My father, Charles McKinley Hindman, was born in 1897. His parents died when he was 3 years old. He was raised by his uncle and we never knew any of his family. He was of German descent and he went into the military during World War I. He met Elsie Ella Thomas and they married. She was raised in Coffeeville, Kansas and was of Indian descent. Her mother, Belle Thomas, was married to Will Thomas and they had four kids. Charles and Elsie married and had thirteen kids, one child died at birth, one died at one year old, and one died at three years old with pneumonia. So, they raised ten kids- five boys and five girls. I am C.M. Hindman, and I was born in Oklahoma on August 30th, 1925. The night I was born, my parents had been to a dance and later that night my mom went into labor and I was delivered by a preacher. He was a mid-wife, that's what they were called.

Early Memories

I was a very busy and curious little boy. My mother said that one time when I was a youngster, I was crawling and some paper had come loose from the wall and some baby mice fell on the floor. My mother took one from my hand, and as she looked closer, she noticed that it had teeth marks on it. Another time, when I was a little older, my Mother had some baby chicks she was raising. I got ahold of one and I put it in water. When she asked me about it, I told her, "I'm baptizing it!"

We left Oklahoma in 1929 and went to New Mexico following construction jobs. Along the way, my father worked on a motel. They had to stand in a soup line a mile long and one day this truck driver came by with a big load of lettuce, and he threw some off for them. Another time, I was scratching around in a junk pile and found a dime. We left New Mexico and headed to Arizona. I let my mother have my dime to buy a gallon of water for the family. Dad worked a little doing odd jobs along the way.

We were camping on the side of the road on our way from Arizona to Arkansas. I was playing around in this field and I found a little boy's hat and I really wanted that hat, but my mother made me put it back where I found it. There had been some migrant workers in the field and she said they would be back and she was afraid I might get head lice, so, I put it back. My brother and I found a rat's nest in the fence and we pulled them out by their tails and one balled up on my hand and bit it. My mother doctored it up and I went back to fight the rats.

We ended up in Arkansas, where my mother had a brother. In the excitement when we got there, someone closed the car door on my thumb and I had a really sore hand for a while. We moved into a house they called, "the house upon the hill", in Mulberry, Arkansas. It had an old smoke house on it and there was an old rusty dish pan lying beside the house. We were playing follow the leader and I fell off the house on the dish pan and cut a gash in my arm. Mom mixed soot out of the cook stove with coal oil and doctored my arm.

The House on the Hill

My Dad got a check from the Army for $300 and he bought 2 cows and a mule and harnesses. The mule's name was Jim, and we took him to green pasture land to graze. We would pull hair from his tail and tie it onto horse flies. Jim got mad and stepped on my brother's toe and bit his leg! We took the cows down to the meadow to graze and we heard an owl and it scared us. My brothers climbed a tree and I couldn't even reach the first limb.

We moved down the hill to another house and Uncle Bill moved up the hill into the house we moved out of. There was a burned out tree stump on the way to get water and one night, Uncle Bill was going after water and saw this stump, and he thought it was a dog and kicked it and broke his toe. The house we moved in down the hill was a bigger, nicer place with a garden spot and fruit trees. We got 300 baby chicks and raised them in a tent. We ate the rooster and kept the hen's to lay eggs so we could eat and sell some. We were working in the garden and I went to the house to get water and I came down with a high fever and passed out under a tree before I got back to the garden with the water. My mother found me unconscious and her and my dad carried me to the house. I was in a coma for several weeks. The doctor said it was Typhoid fever. He told them to keep me comfortable and get my fever down, and I would have a 50% chance of living. He directed them to get a wash tub and fill it with water, and chip up a 25lb block of ice and put me in it, and give me no solid food. I was five years old at the time. My fever broke but I had a chigger bite in the top of my head and I had to wear gloves because I dug at the bite and nearly dug a hole in my scalp. Someone sat up with me day and night until my fever broke. One evening, my dad had some mules in the back yard grazing and they were tied up in the yard. They got tangled up in the wire and started bucking and broke loose and the family left the table to catch the mules and I got to the table and ate two rolls and that caused a setback. I was down again for six weeks, but, I finally got over the illness.

Grandpa worked for the railroad and every summer Grandma would ride the train from Kansas and come spend the summer with us. She would bring her featherbed in a trunk, and all us kids couldn't wait for her to come and we would fight over who's turn it would be to sleep with her in that bed. That was quite a treat! Grandma smoked a red clay pipe made by the Indians with RJ Reynolds tobacco, the strongest you could get at the time. I would help her light her pipe with a very small coal I pinched out of the fireplace between my thumb and forefinger. Grandma would ask me, "how can you do that?" I told her, "well, it is very hot, so you have to be quick."

This is back when we lived on the hill. One day, my dad made some peach brandy. My mom and dad went off to town and he came back drunk and he hit Mother in the head and made it bleed. My sisters wanted to kill him. Then my dad rode a horse up in the mountains and met up with this man with a Jenny and I guess he traded my dad "home brew" for the Jenny. That man had a drinking problem and he must have been mean to the Jenny because she was mean too. She would either lay down with you on her, or throw you off.

On the Move Again

After I got over the fever and school started, the older kids started to school, but they didn't get to go very long because my dad moved again. We were home schooled by our mother most of our school years. We moved and while moving, the wagon turned over and my baby sister was under a lot of stuff, but we found her and she was unhurt. We had a little dog and he ran off when that happened and we never found him again. We finally made it to the house. Dad went off to a sale and came home with a goat. My brother and I decided we would make a harness for the goat. So, we took my dad's razor and cut some binding with the eyelets in it off the tent that we used to raise the chickens in so we could make the harness. We used an old cultivator for the cart. The next morning, when our dad went to shave, he screamed, "who has had my razor?!" He used his razor strap to fix the razor, and then he strapped us with it too! It was my idea, but my brother got strapped too. We ended up killing the goat and eating it not too long after.

Fetchin' and Playin'

When I was eight years old we moved again to
Lonelum. We had to cross a swinging bridge to go to
school. My mother sent me to the store to get a gallon of
kerosene. It cost a nickel. On the way back, I hit the
gallon jar on a rock and broke it. She wasn't too upset
and sent me back to the store with a jug and a dozen eggs
to pay for the kerosene. I was extra careful and made it
safely back with that jar. While living there, someone
before us had planted some tobacco and my brother and I
took some of the leaves and dried them out and then
crushed them. Then we put them in a skillet and put

them in the fire place so they would crush better. We rolled us some tobacco and my older sister was curious. So we talked her into smoking some and she got sick and went out and lay in the front porch. When our parents came home, my mother said, "What in the world is wrong with you?" She was pale and sick as she could be. She said, "The boys made me do it!" She never smoked again in her life- that was enough for her.

Fishin' and Playin'

My dad and some men got together and went to
the river to fish. They had a real good catch so they
divided the fish up and we had a fish fry. So my mother
invited her brother and his wife to come over and eat. My
uncle got choked on a fish bone and we thought he was
going to die. They liked to have never got it out. It scared
us kids to death. We didn't even want to eat fish and
some won't eat fish still today. My mother said, "See what
happens if you don't pay attention to what you are doing."
I was trying to act silly like I was choking and my dad

made me leave the table. My mother came to see about

me later and she brought me some fish and a biscuit.

Sweet Sorghum

There was a sorghum syrup mill in the community and everyone took their cane there to make sorghum. A mule would go round and round this thing they put the cane in and squeeze the juice out. They had a big metal trough, eight to ten feet long and about 2 foot wide, that they cooked it in, and they would put it in a gallon bucket to take home. We looked forward to that.

Learning About Life, and Death

Prior to this place, we lived where we had a lot of chickens. We were taking them to market and a lot of them got hot and smothered to death. So, we dressed them and took them home and had fried chicken!

We went to this man's house that lived close to the river and some of the kids were playing in the water. So, my brother got in and got on this log, and it started rolling over and over with him and he almost drowned. They had to pull him out. Later, I went to play with these kids at their house. Their grandmother had died and the kids were excited because they were going to get to play the

Victrola at her funeral. The kids also said they were going

to bury her in the garden.

Hog Shorts and Blackberry Cobbler

We made some stilts and had fun trying to walk on those stilts. I went in the house and told Momma the roof was on fire. She was cooking supper and said, "Son, go on and stop playing around." My brother came in and said, "Momma, the roof is on fire." I said, "I tried to tell you!" and we started pouring water on it and finally put it out.

Dad went off to Little Rock, Arkansas to try and get his pension started at the VA and was gone for a week. All we had to eat were eggs and milk, no bread. So mom used hog shorts to make flap jacks. She didn't have any coffee or anything to cook when he came home. He had a little money and she got flour, meal, lard, and coffee.

My brother and I were making a sled and we were putting runners on it. I let it fall on his leg and he got mad and ran after me. He hung his neck on a clothesline wire and that really made him mad! When he caught me, he beat up on me.

Momma and I went to pick blackberries. I was on this log and a big black snake came down the log and I had to jump in the vine or over the snake. So, I jumped the snake and we got a bucket full of berries and momma made a cobbler.

Careful What You Ask For

The next day or so, my mom and dad were shucking some feed by hand using a machete and then they would wrap it up and tie it, and stand it up with the grain inside to protect it from the rain. I was supposed to take them some water. Meantime, I was playing around with some farm equipment and my sister that followed me, like a shadow all the time, was there with me. I saw these wasps in one of the pipes and I told her to blow on one end and when they came out, I would kill them. But, the wasp went out her end and stung her on the lips and they swelled and turned wrong side out. All you could see was her teeth. I told her not to follow me to take the water, but she did and momma said, "Oh, what is wrong with your mouth?" Momma had to go to the house and doctor her, and gave me a whipping. I went to the house and got on the front porch. There was a fishing pole lying there and I saw a wasp nest up in the corner of the porch. I picked up the fishing pole and said, "I wish I would get stung". I picked up the nest with the fishing pole and one came right down the pole and stung me under the eye, and my eye swelled too!

Hunting, Fishing, and the Mumps

We were all in bed and we heard all these dogs barking. They kept getting closer and closer, and our house set up at the back a little more than the front. This man was fox hunting and the dogs chased a fox under the house. They ran under one side and out the other and the next morning there was blood in the yard from the dogs' feet running on the rocks.

The next day or so, dad and I went down to a little creek to fish. I was fishing with a pole and I caught a fish. I jerked so hard that I hung it in a tree. Dad was fishing with three way hook, but he didn't catch anything. So, I climbed the tree and got my fish and threw it back in since we didn't have enough fish to cook.

My brother and I went fishing. We must have walked a mile and on the way, we crossed a watermelon patch. So, we got us one and put it in the water to get cool. When we cut it open, it was green. So, we were hungry and ate it, and then didn't feel good. We went home and we both had fever. We came down with the mumps.

Chicks, Chicken Pox, and Biscuits in a Shoe

Momma sent me under the house to get some eggs a hen had laid near the hearth of the fireplace where it was warm. But when she broke one in the skillet, it had started making a chick! It had been under there too long.

That same year we all had the measles and we all had the chicken pox too. The other kids got everything from school. I was home-schooled because I was sick so much. And, my mother didn't want me picking up any viruses from other kids. But the older kids brought it all home to me anyway.

My sister got some new shoes and I was mad because I didn't get any. So, I stuffed a biscuit in the toe of her shoe and the dog tried to get it and tore her shoe up. I got a whipping.

On the Move Again

While we were in Arkansas, momma had a boy and then a still born baby girl, and then another boy. So when we left Arkansas, there were eight kids. So, how did we all get in the Model A pickup truck? We had to pull a little trailer for our stuff. When the baby girl was still born, momma took the pneumonia and she had breast fever. So, I went to a neighbor's house and borrowed a breast pump. I was eight years old.

The Cheatum Place

We moved to another place we called the Cheatum place. It was 120 acres. We had a brother born on that place. We were getting ready that fall to move into our final place before we came to Texas. We moved on to 120 acres that had an orchard and farming land. We were able to make a pretty good living on it. We moved on this place, but my dad and sisters had gone to Texas the year before and picked cotton and did pretty well. So, he wanted us all to come to Texas and make money to pay on this place. But we had to stay to finish the crops we had already started. When we put the crop in, my brother and I was the hired hands. Dad was going to town and he said we could go to the movies. So he came to the field and hollered and my brother said, "What did he say?" I said, "I think he said run the mules." So, he started running the mules. I saw him cut a switch and I said, "I think he said don't run the mules. I think we are in trouble." Sure enough, we both got a whipping. We still went to town and we saw these people going in this place. Nobody came out. We said, "What are they doing?" Dad said, "They are going to the movie." This was the first one we had ever gone to and it was a silent one. People would laugh and we would laugh too, but we didn't know why. When we got out of the movie, we got a hamburger and a Coke. When we started to go home, he had some groceries and he had some Miller High Life beer.

Fried Pies, Quilts, and Skips

We were drying peaches on top of the house on a sheet. We broke the peaches open and took the seed out, and laid them with the meat side up and let the sun dry them. Then momma would store them and in the winter, she could make cobblers and fried pies out of them. She was a very good cook.

In the spring, my sisters loaded our winter quilts in the little red wagon and took them to the creek and put them in upstream and laid rocks on them so they wouldn't wash away while the water rippled over them and washed them. My brother and I were supposed to load them up that afternoon and take them to the house. But, we got to playing and running down the creek and all the sudden, we realized it was dusty dark. So, we thought about the quilts and started running back to get them. But, when we got there, they were gone. We thought they had washed away. So, we started running down the creek looking for them, but we couldn't find them. It was getting dark, so we went to the house looking to get the whipping of our life. But when we got to the house, the girls had gone back and got the quilts. They were hanging on the line to dry. Boy, were we ever happy to see those quilts!

Our dad had given my brother and me about a half-gallon of peas and told us to plant them in the skips in the corn field. We planted about half of them, and we thought if we told him we had some left, he would make us plant them someplace else. So, we saw this old hollow tree and decided to pour them in the hollow tree, not thinking what would happen if it rained (there was a hole in the bottom). Sure enough, it did rain and washed the peas all down the creek bed. Weeks later, he decided to take us fishing down this creek. There was a good fishing spot, and he saw all these peas that had come up along the way and he was trying to figure out where they came from. We slid by on that one.

Fishin' and Freezin'

In April of that spring, my dad, brother and I, and my dad's friend and his son went fishing. It was five miles or more from home. We boys were bare footed. It had been warm but after we got there, a front moved in and it turned cold and started snowing. There was an old house there with part of the roof off and we got in there for a little cover. My dad tore some wood off the old house and built a fire in an old fireplace. We hadn't taken much cover to make beds, so we almost froze to death. It was too cold to catch any fish, but we had some eggs and bacon for breakfast that we took with us. So, we decided to go home. It was a trip we would remember and next time, we would go more prepared.

Outlaw Camp

Before we left Arkansas in 1935, my dad and uncle
went hunting. Me and my brother went along but we just
prowled around while they hunted. We found this old
cave and we went on top of the cave and looked in. It
looked like someone had camped there. The story was
that outlaws used to camp there. Our dog ran in the cave
and came out yipping. We didn't stay there long! On the
way home, my brother was carrying a shot gun. I said I
had never shot a shotgun. My dad said, "Let him shoot it,
but it will kick you real hard." So, I backed up against a
tree and it kicked and I hurt my shoulder because it had

no place to go. I never wanted to shoot it any more. It wasn't as much fun as I thought it would be.

Heading to Texas to Pick Cotton

A few days later, in late summer or early fall, my dad had been talking to someone in Texas about picking cotton. We were supposed to get there by the time the cotton was ready to pick. The night before we left, my brother and I went down the road to borrow a lantern so we could see how to catch the chickens after they went to roost. A man was coming to buy the chickens and we had to put them in cages for him. We sold everything we had to get enough money to leave Arkansas and come to Texas. On the way home with the lantern, my brother and I heard this owl. It was a sound like we had never heard. It sounded like a woman screaming to us. It scared us to death! We ran as fast as we could, our hearts pounding! But, we didn't say anything to our dad. The next morning we got up early and momma cooked breakfast and we all ate and she washed the dishes. We started packing up the trailer dad would pull behind the Model-A pickup. We packed bedding, pots and pans, dishes, and everything we needed to cook with, our clothes and stuff we needed, potatoes, onions and eggs, some ham we had from killing a hog, some fruit and other food momma had canned. We left about ten o'clock and we drove until one or two o'clock. We stopped and momma fixed lunch at this road side park because we could get water there to cook, and a bath, and use the bathroom. So, we just camped there for the night and that gave us kids time to run around and get some exercise. We would meet people and some would be going to Arkansas and other places looking for work. The next morning momma fixed us some breakfast and we loaded up and got on our way. There was more to road side parks back then. Sometimes we would see people traveling in covered wagons. It took us several days to make the trip. We came thru Hugo, Oklahoma and crossed the red river and came into Paris, Texas. That night we stayed in a motel in Paris. Momma found a laundry mat where she could wash our clothes the next day.

RC Cola and the Spotted Pony

We left Paris and went to Deport, Texas. All the way from Arkansas to Texas I would ask my dad, "Is it time to stop and get a RC Cola?" He said, "I'll stop when I think it's time." There was a little station between Paris and Deport and he stopped and got us a RC Cola. My dad and my older sisters had been to Deport a couple of years before to pick cotton, so they knew where we were going. They had told us that these people had a spotted pony and we couldn't wait to see this pony. But we didn't like him when we met him because he would bite us, and we

decided we didn't want to have anything to do with this
pony, spots or no spots.

Setting Up House and Tasting Success

We went to see the man that we had picked cotton for and he told my dad he didn't have a decent place for a family to stay. So we stayed that night in what seemed to be a chicken house and the next day he told my dad about this farmer that needed some help. So we went to Deport, Texas and his farm was just outside Deport. When we got there he had a two bedroom house for us to stay in and we got what we needed to set up housekeeping. He had lots of cotton so my dad bought cotton sacks for the older kids and I had to use a tow-sack. The two younger sisters stayed home to help my mother with the two younger brothers. Even at my young age, I wondered why we kept getting more brothers and sisters when my dad couldn't take care of the ones we had. They had three while we lived in Arkansas and two more after we came to Texas. So, we picked cotton all fall and made quite a bit of money.

Dad traded the little truck for a bigger truck to haul all our stuff back to Arkansas where we came from because we had made a down payment on the 120 acres and the man just wanted $1600 for it so we were going back to try and pay for the farm. He was checking the truck over and he had taken the battery cable off and it fell off the stabilizer bar and cut the gas line and it set the truck on fire and it burned to the ground. It was so hot it even burned the tires off. It would have set the house on fire too if it had been a little closer to the house. The man that we had been picking cotton for felt so bad for us that he told my dad he had this little place in the country that we could live on and share crop on it for one-third of the crop. He got a fourth and he furnished us a wagon and a team of mules and the farm equipment and the seeds that we needed to plant.

Tough Soles

When we lived in Glendale, we had to make pallets on the floor to try and find a cool place to sleep. We had rats and we always went bare footed and our feet were so tough that at night the rats would try to eat callouses off of our heels.

The older kids started to school in Glendale, it was almost mid-term. They had to walk thru the woods three miles to school. One of the boys had it in for the mean teacher. This teacher had a tennis shoe with the top cut off and he would whip the boys with that shoe sole. On April Fool's Day, he threw the school bell in the toilet. But in the summer, they cleaned the toilet out and found the bell and someone told who did it. When school started again, he made the boy wear it around his neck for half a day.

Getting the Cotton to Market

While living in Glendale, we had three bales of
cotton in the barn and my dad, me, and my brother
helped load them on a flatbed wagon. We had no way to
tie them down, and they were standing on end. We left
that road and were turning onto another road that was an
incline and the wagon listed and one bale fell off the
wagon. So, my brother and I had to turn the wagon
around and get the back of the wagon lower so we could
get the end of the bale on the edge of the wagon, and push
it back on the wagon. This was a job that should have
been impossible to do at our size. But we managed to do

it, and took them on into town. Someone unloaded them

for us and we left them until the cotton buyer came to

town. He would grade the cotton according to the stable

of the cotton and buy according to the quality of the

cotton. So we went on back home. It was about 7 miles

and it took us about four hours or a half a day.

Got Cows?

One Sunday morning the first weekend we were there, we were outside under a tree and this man rode up on a horse and asked my dad if he had any cows so he could have milk for us kids, and he said no, I haven't been able to get one yet. The man said, "I live down the road about a mile and a half, come down to my house and get some cows." So we got three cows, one had a calf by her side, and the other two had weaned their calves. So we had all the milk and butter we needed. I did most of the milking, at ten years old. The man that lent us the cows had two granddaughters and one of them had a car wreck and was paralyzed for life- so sad. The cows he let us use

he said he wanted the bull calves to sell and that we could

keep the heifers to grow a herd.

Dotting the "I"

The first Christmas we were there, 1935, dad got his VA pension started. So we had some money for Christmas and I got a BB gun and later we got a bicycle together. But, my brother rode it on a muddy road and warped the wheel and we couldn't ride it any more. So dad bought a 22 rifle and that was my brother's, and the BB gun was mine. But my brother used so many shells that my dad took the gun from him. He was shooting everything. My dad took the gun to hunt squirrels and rabbits in the winter. We had plenty of meat then.

One Sunday morning, some of the kids were going to Sunday school, but I didn't go because I wanted to go hunting. I found this junk pile and there was an old Ohio crock in the junk. I was going to dot the "i" in Ohio, and the BB came back and hit me in the eye, and I couldn't see. I managed to get to the fence and I followed it to the cross fence, and I followed it home. I went in the back door and got on my bed and my mother heard me and she came in and said, "Son, what's wrong?" I said, "I shot my eye". It was bleeding and she looked and she had a fit. She sent one of the kids to find my dad. He was down the road drinking home brew with some men and he started home and was running so much that he fainted. Meantime, someone had gone to town to get the doctor and when he came, he had to doctor my dad too. My eyes crossed, and I couldn't see for eight weeks. So that's another reason my mom home schooled me, because I was always sick or getting hurt. Finally, my eyes corrected their self.

A few days later, the pasture across the road caught on fire and my family was all out there trying to help put it out. I could smell the smoke and I still was not seeing too good. So I crossed the road and went out into the woods and the smoke was so thick it got in my eyes and I couldn't see. I was screaming and my mother found me and took me back home and told me not to get out again. I had worked on her last nerve. She didn't know what to expect from me next.

Days later, my mom and dad had gone to town to get some groceries and momma always read to us at night. She had read a story about a cowboy. So while they were gone to town, my brother took a rope off the plow that we used to work the garden and made a bull rope. My brother tied me on this calf and turned it loose. He ran down to the woods into a thorn bush and one of those thorns caught me in the ear and almost tore a hole in my ear. My sisters doctored my ear. It was bleeding and when momma came home she said, "What in the world is going to happen to you next?"

Tackle Crafting

We met this man up town that worked in the hardware store. He was fascinated by us five boys getting our hair cut and he wanted to come out and fish in our stock tank. One day on his day off, he came out to fish. He had a rod and reel and he took the line off and put a new line on. He gave me the spool of old line and I got me a piece of cane pole and put the spool on it. I cut a hole in the cane pole and put stove bolts and put a wing nut and left it so I could turn it. I made eyelets on the cane pole and I put the line on the spool and made me a rod and reel. Everyone thought that was real smart that I could do that. I made a lure out of a piece of wood and I whittled it with my pocket knife to look like a fish. I could catch fish with it. Everyone thought that was something else.

My Next Invention

I caught two dry land turtles and I drilled a hole in their shell, front and back, and tied them together. Then I cut a hole in the back of the shells on the other side of each turtle and took twine string and attached it to a match box. I would fill the box with sand and watch them pull the box. It made a great toy and I would play with them for hours. My brother and cousin were playing with me and they left and I didn't know where they went. My uncle had just moved in down the road from us. They were making their way to California and weren't going to be living here long. My cousin didn't want to go to

California, so my brother and cousin decided to run off. They went to Deport, Texas, to catch the train. My uncle found out and came and got my dad and they followed the train until it stopped and they got the boys. My dad almost beat my brother to death with a belt.

Excitement in the Community

My sister was just like my shadow. She followed me to the barn to milk and I told her, "Look, this utter does not have a hole in it." When she looked, I squirted milk in her face and she ran to the house crying. I got a whipping. That's what my dad did best, every time anything happened.

After that, we had a lot of excitement in the community. This man that lived on a farm nearby kept saying he was going to kill someone and everyone was scared. His wife was pregnant and he killed her and the baby with his pocket knife, and they sent him to prison.

Prior to that, my dad came in drunk and he was scared too. So he made all us kids get up and line up around the wall and he got his automatic rifle that held twenty one shells and said he was going to shoot the first one that came down the road. He went outside and the man that had scared everyone came by and my dad started shooting in the air. It scared us to death, especially my mom. She was pregnant at the time and it scared the man because he drove as fast as he could.

Snakes and Honey

The second crop we made on the farm was corn. One morning my brother and I went to get the mules up and we heard this rattlesnake by this tree. My brother said, "You watch him and I'll run to the house and get the gun." When he came back, the snake was gone. I didn't see where he went, but when we went to work in the corn field, he was there. My dad killed him throwing corn at him. He had seven rattlers and was six foot long.

That weekend my brother and I were fishing and I was catching grasshoppers to fish with. I found a little grass snake and I put it in my tobacco sack. My brother had a tobacco can and he asked me for some tobacco. He was holding his paper in his hand and watching his cork and I dumped that snake on his tobacco paper. He jumped up and the chase was on. Meantime, some woodcutters had come in to cut wood. They had a tent and they would leave on the weekend. So my dad went in the tent and scratched on it and growled and it scared us to death. We forgot about the snake and took off as fast as we could. Dad came out and hollered at us and was laughing.

That fall, my older sister got married. I think she was seventeen. Her husband didn't act any older than us. He still liked to play cowboys just like us and liked to run down the creek and climb trees. I found this old tree down by the creek that had honey bees in it and I told dad. Him and a neighbor went down to the creek and broke a limb off. It was full of honey comb. We got about 2 gallons of strained honey, but the neighbor got covered with bees and he ran and jumped in the pool. I stood back to watch but they started after me and I was fighting

them with my cap. I put my cap on and one got in my hair

and I liked to have never gotten him out.

The Lil' Banty

Dad came home with two turkey hens and they had been laying and dad sent us to find their nest but they were setting and they made a blowing sound so we left them. But, I found a quail's nest with 16 eggs and the quail was off so I put them in my hat and took them home. I put them under a banty hen. All 16 hatched. Some stayed around and some left. The little banty couldn't figure out why her babies could fly and she couldn't. We went back and were able to get the baby turkeys and brought them home and the momma came looking for them and that's how we caught her.

Tough Times in Rosalie

We bought our own team of mules and we moved
to another place east of Bogota to the community named
Rosalie. We thought it was a good place but it had a lot of
alkali in the dirt and it wouldn't grow cotton. We sowed
some Sudan grass and made some hay and that's about all
we got out of it. We went to school there, and there were
five of us that were school age. Our mother would make
bread and fix our lunch. We would walk about a mile and
a half to school and on the weekends, we would pick
cotton for other farmers. That's the only way we made
any money that year. Dad did day labor and he was

drawing his pension check. Me and my brother had to cut wood for our mother to cook with and to keep warm that winter by the wood stove. The lady that owned the place told us we could only cut the dead limbs. We said, "We only get to cut the rotten ones that are no good?" and she said, "Beggars can't be choosers." We told our dad what she said and he went to confront her and she met him with a shotgun, and said she would shoot him. My mother called him back, said it's not worth it.

On a brighter side, my mom and dad had gone to town in this old car he bought and left us kids home. We took a rope and tied it around my little brother's waist and up thru his overall, and hung him up on the pole across from the entrance to the barn. When they came home, my dad had had a drink or two and it scared him so bad he ran into the corner of the house and we really got in trouble for that. We thought it would be funny, but they didn't think so. It was 1938.

Back To Glendale and Hard Times

The following Sunday, my brother went to a ball game and wanted me to go but I didn't go. He met this man that was from Arkansas where we had lived and he got in the car and went back to Arkansas with him. He was gone about a week and my mother got a card from this lady we knew and told her he was there. He came back home and didn't get in too much trouble for going. Not long after he got back, we moved back to Glendale where we had lived before next door to the school. There was no farming land there, but there was pasture for the cows and horses we had, and a good lake. We had to go down in the bottom to farm. Prior to moving there, we went there on the weekend to see who owned it. A friend of my dad had lived there and he was moving back to where he had lived. We had Sunday dinner with them and then we went back home. We were in a wagon and the next weekend we moved. This man who owned it lived out west and he said we could live there just for cutting brush and cleaning the place up.

But meantime, the Civilian Conservation Corps (C.C.C.) came in and cleaned the place up and my brother joined the C.C.C. and he went to East Texas. We made a couple of crop before my brother joined the C.C.C. and I had to drop out of school in 1941 to help make a living for the family. My sisters all had a hard time too. When it was time to wash clothes, they fetched wood and built a fire to heat the water in the wash pot and scrubbed the clothes on the rub board, then hung them on the clothes line and along the fence. They also helped mom with cooking and cleaning and then picked cotton and worked in the field. The whole family worked hard.

One day we were out on the front porch playing and scuffling around and one of my sisters started screaming and crying. With no questions asked, my dad came out and grabbed the spring off the door and warped me across the bare back with it and it left marks on my back where that spring pinched my skin. I can't begin to tell you the thoughts that went through my mind.

One of my sisters graduated while we lived there and she married a boy that went to school with her and they stayed in Bogota for a while, and then they moved to Dallas.

While we lived there, we had straw mattresses and then the community had a home demonstration agent come and the women got together and she showed them how to make cotton mattresses. Each family made three and they had springs too. The Federal Government furnished the cotton and the women made the ticks and stuffed them to make the mattresses. The next year, we moved to a new place across the road. It was sandy land and that's where we grew a big garden, three or four acres. We grew everything we could.

My Horse

I went to the bank and borrowed some money to buy a horse from the man that gave us the cows to milk. I broke the horse to ride and he turned out to be a good saddle horse. I let my dad borrow him to ride to town. My dad got drunk and the constable tried to pull him off the horse and he did, and he took him to jail. The constable just turned the horse loose, and he came back home. Then the heifers got out and went down in the bottom and I rode my horse to get them and he got into some loco weeds and ate some and they made him crazy. I could never ride him again. So, I traded him for a gentle horse and some pigs and a wind charger so we could have

a radio. I left the gentle horse there for the kids to ride.

A man gave me a patch of cotton to pull the bolls and I

pulled the bolls and paid for my horse. I took the bolls to

the gin and I sold the seeds and the cotton.

Splitting My Toe

Before my brother left to go to the CC Camp, some limbs had blown onto the farm land. We were using a chopping axe to cut them and my brother sharpened my axe during lunch because I told him it was dull. When we went to cut the limb, the first one I cut the axe went through the limb and I split my left big toe. I had on rubber boots and I was bleeding real bad. I walked about three miles back to the house, and went in the back door so my mother couldn't see it. She was pregnant and my older sister was there and she doctored it before my mother saw it. Later that evening, my dad got home and they took me to town to the doctor but it had swollen and he couldn't sew it up. He had to put clamps to close it. He put seven clamps on it. I went back one time to get it dressed and it hurt so bad because he didn't deaden it or anything. He said he would take the clamps out when it was ready. But I had decided I would take them out myself. I put the point of my mother's barber scissors in the clamp, and spread them apart, and I pulled all the clamps out myself. My sister doctored it for me. I'm almost ninety years old and I still have the scar.

Looking In the Rear-View Mirror

My brother joined the army in 1941 during WWII. He was stationed in Sherman, Texas so he would come home some weekends. One weekend he got married. Sometimes his wife would stay a few days with us and one time I was taking her back to her mother's and we had to go this dirt road and we went through this area where Indians once lived. There were these big mounds that they used to set their tents on so the water would drain off and they just cut this road through this area. It was rough and steep and my car wouldn't go, so I told her to get in the driver's seat and I would push and when I told her to gas it, go and then let off on it. When we got to the top part she didn't let off and my front wheel hit the side of one of these mounds and locked and we couldn't go. So, I had to walk home through the woods and my dad got the mules and we went back and he tied on to the wheel and got it straight. There was no place to turn around, so I had to go way out of the way to get home, and she walked on to her mother's.

I traded that car for a Model A with 4 doors. Daddy and a couple of his friends wanted to go to town and I took them. It started raining and rained all day and coming home they had been drinking and all three were in the back seat passing the bottle around. The one that was sitting behind me kept hitting me in the back of the head with his hat because it made me mad to get my hair messed up. I told him three times to quit. I was having a hard time keeping the car on the road it was so muddy. When I got to a sandy spot where I could stop, I stopped and opened the door and jerked him out and landed him flat on his back in the middle of the road. I told him that was not half of what he was going to get if he did it again. My dad said, "I told you he's got a temper." He was about my size and I think I made a believer out of him and the other two laughed at him. When I got them home, that was their last trip to ride with me.

One night I drove my car to town and I parked it under the water tower so I could push it off. Someone relieved himself in my radiator and after the show I was taking these two girls home. One of them was spending the night with the other one. When my car heated up, it smelled like urine and they didn't know if I had wet my pants and I didn't know if they had wet theirs. I never found out who did it- no one would own up to it.

Shortly after that, I traded for a Model A Coupe and these soldiers came down from Paris and wanted to go buy some home brew. I knew where to take them because I knew where my dad got home brew and they would pay me to take them to get the home brew. I came up with the idea that I could get it on my way into town and I wouldn't have to make a trip back to get it when they came down. I only did it a couple or three times and I decided that was bootlegging and I wasn't going to do that anymore, so that Saturday night I took a girl to the show. A week or so later, I went to town and someone told the constable I was bootlegging. I pulled up and parked behind the domino hall and the constable walked up and stuck a gun in the car and told me to get out. He and my dad had got in a fight before. My dad whipped him and he jerked my dad off my horse and turned it loose and my horse came home. He made me get out of the car and he took the seat out and opened the rumble seat and took the cotton sack out and the seat and threw it all on the ground and left it and went back in the domino hall. I went in and the City Judge was playing dominoes and he said, "How are you son?" I said, "I wish you would come and see what the constable just did to my car." He told him to put everything back like it was and he told the man that ran the domino hall to go see that he did it.

I was taking the kids to the cotton patch in my car because the wagon was already in the field with cotton in it and I was going to pick too, but it had rained and then dried up and the road was rough. I hit high center and it drug my battery off. So a neighbor took me to town to get a battery. When we got back to the house, I went to the barn and got a tow sack to put my battery in to carry my battery back to the car, and slung it over my back and then put it in my car. I put my cotton sack on and started picking cotton and my back started burning. The acid had eaten my cotton sack and shirt and some of my pants. It even ate the seat cover because the acid had run out when I was carrying it. I went down to the levy and washed off and tied my cotton sack around me and went to the house. Mom fixed me some vinegar water to bathe in. I even had to put a new seat cover on my car seat. I had to borrow a cotton sack to finish our crop. Then we went to pick cotton for someone else and I didn't have a sack. So the man we were picking for said he would go to the house and get me a sack. While he was gone, I picked cotton and left it in the row and when he got back, I put it in my sack and we weighed up and I had more than anyone else.

Later that fall, I took my dad to town to get groceries and he got drunk and wanted to stop at this little store on the way home. We didn't need anything but I stopped and I kept telling him we needed to go. He said, "We'll go when I get ready." He bought half dozen eggs and threw them on my car and I just drove off and left him. When I got home, my mom asked, "Where is your dad?" I told her I left him and told her what he did. I cleaned my car and went back to town another way and he walked home and never mentioned it to me.

Going to the Grocer

After we came to Texas and when I was eleven years old, I would get up and do my chores and eat breakfast. I would hook the mules to the wagon and go seven miles to get groceries for my mother and she would always tell me, "now you get yourself something to eat." I would get a sleeve of crackers and half pound of bologna because I loved bologna, and a drink. I liked red soda pop because they were big. I liked the most for my money. It took about four hours to make the trip. They would always put the ticket in a box and every month they had a drawing for a war bond. They would always put my name on the ticket but I never won until I was older. I let my

dad have it to cash in. It was $16.75 and all I ever got was

a bridle rein that cost about $1.50. I don't know what he

did with the rest, but I have a good idea it was spent on

booze.

The Woodpecker

One day it was snowing and I saw this woodpecker outside going round and round this tree. I said, "I'm going to catch that bird." My dad said, "You can't catch that bird." So I watched him and when he got on the back side, I opened the door and stepped out on the porch. Every time he went to the back side of the tree, I would move a little closer and I did that until I got up to the tree. He was on the side and when he got to the back of the tree, I reached around and grabbed him. I held him up to show him I caught him. I took him in the house and he was kicking and making a sound to try and get loose. So, I took him out and let him go. That same day, my younger brother got one leg hung in this chair and he fell against the heater and slid one cheek down that hot stove and burned it. He let out a screaming cry. My mother put butter on it and she kept it dry where he couldn't scratch it and it didn't leave a scar.

Life Lesson

Back when I was young and living on the farm, if an animal died, you would drag it off usually to a brush pile and later it could be burned. So one day my baby brother came in the house and told my mother a neighbor had died and she asked him how he knew and he told her one of the other neighbors told him. She asked how did he know and my little brother said, "I don't know, guess he saw them dragging him off." Then my mother had to explain to him the difference when it was a person.

Signing Up!

One morning after breakfast, we got all our cotton picking stuff. I was taking my brothers and sisters to the field to pick cotton and we were playing around a little. We were in the wagon and I rubbed the post at the gate and my dad saw it. He was working in the garden and he came over and took the check line and warped me across the back with it. I just crawled down off the wagon and I said that's the last time you will ever hit me. I went to the house and told my mother I was going to town and signing up for the next draft. She cried but she understood. So I went and signed up and they took me shortly and sent me to California. There were several of us that they sent to San Diego, California for boot camp. I felt guilty for leaving my sisters and little brothers behind but I felt like I had to go before something bad happened. I wrote my mother twice, sometime three times a week and gave her a progress report. She looked forward to hearing from me. She would read the letters to my sisters and brothers at night and they would cry. My dad would say, "What the hell are you crying for?" One of my sisters was pretty vocal and she would say, "If you don't know, you are crazy." When we got to California and got fitted for our clothes and shoes, they gave me shoes two sizes too big. The first time we went out on the grinder learning to march and semi-formation, I had blisters on top of blisters on my feet and I had to go to sick bay. The doctor said, "Who issued you these shoes? I'm going to have a talk with them." They gave me some shoes that fit.

While I was in boot camp, I learned that Jerry Lewis and Gene Kelly were in boot camp too, but they weren't in our unit. Our unit was made up mostly with boys from Texas and Oklahoma. There were at least two hundred of us. We finished boot camp and on Thanksgiving Day, I had to go to the dentist. The ones that had tobacco stains on them, they drilled them out and filled them, said they were cavities, but they weren't. In later years, I lost every one of them. I always said they just did it for identification. They told me not to eat or drink anything hot or cold. That didn't leave me much to eat on Thanksgiving Day.

We won the barracks pennant and it was issued for cleanness. We also won the rowing pennant. We were in this big rowboat with about sixteen men on each side and our company won the race. I also won marksman and that was a campaign ribbon. I won several ribbons while in training. I was a first class marksman and swimmer. We had to learn to do hand to hand combat and learn to shoot rifles, how to throw hand grenades, and how to abandon ship. We learned a lot in boot camp. We learned to wash our clothes properly and how to cook. We learned how to survive. When we went to the separation center, me and my buddy from our home town would always line up side by side because we thought we would go to the same place because they would always pull four from each side. But that time, they did it by twos, and we got separated and didn't see each other again until we got back home. He went to sea and I went to another base in California.

Call From Home

One Sunday afternoon, I was in the movies and I thought I heard someone call my name. I even looked around. It was an intrusion. It was the Red Cross looking for me. My sister was calling for me so the Red Cross was looking for me. My older sister was pregnant and had pneumonia and her husband was on a ship and couldn't be reached. So she was calling for me. She was very ill, and my company commander gave me an emergency leave for a week and I started hitchhiking to North Island. I had to cross a bay and this guy kept following me wanting me to go to a room with him. I was scared and worried about my sister and I told him to go on and leave me alone. He kept following me and we got to a hedge row and I had a bag and I had a sack of pennies in it I was taking to my little sister. I swung that bag around and hit him upside the head and that was the last I saw of him. I had been saving my money up to get a tailor made uniform so I took that money and bought a train ticket to Dallas. When I got to Dallas, I was looking for a road that would take me to Paris, Texas. When I was walking to find the road to Paris, I saw this friend of my sisters walking down the street and she asked me, "Where in the world are you going?" I told her about my sister and she gave me five dollars and told me to go to the bus station and get me a ticket to Paris. I hated to take her money, but I was desperate and that was a blessing that I saw her. I got my bus ticket and went to Paris. I didn't know where she was so I started walking. I was still about twenty five miles from home and this man stopped and picked me up. I told him my story and he had lived in the town where my parents lived at one time, so he took me all the way to my parents' house. My parents still had my car but it wasn't in a very good condition. I did manage to go to Paris the next morning where my sister was. I had used up three days of my leave and I only had seven. I still didn't have any money, so I went to the bank where they knew me and got some money. I got a week's extension on my leave and my sister started getting better.

Back to Serve

I got back to Venetian, California where I left from.
I got back a day early and everyone was gone. They had
moved to Camp Ojai and all my stuff was gone. I didn't
know what I was going to do, but a truck came to pick up
some stuff they had left behind and he told me they
moved to Camp Ojai. I rode back to camp with him and I
asked them where I could find my stuff. They told me
where I was supposed to be, but on the way back to Camp
Ojai, I bought a little bottle of liquor so we could celebrate
my return. My friends didn't know where I had gone and
they were sure glad to see me. They grabbed that bottle

and I never saw it again until it was empty. I never drank any of it. We left Camp Ojai by truck and went to Twenty Nine Palms, California. When we got there, it was way out in the desert.

Didn't much happen there until this guy went home on leave and he brought his car back. It was a '41 Ford 4 door. One weekend he was going to take six guys to L.A. I signed up to go but I didn't get my money that was owed to me from a guy so I didn't go. So they went and some more guys had gone to town in another car. On the way home, they saw this bad wreck and they told the authority and they went to check and it was the car I was supposed to go in. They had hit a sand dune and rolled five or six times and it killed all of them but the driver. Six guys were all out of the car and some couldn't be recognized, but they knew who all was in the car. They asked me if I would volunteer to accompany one of the bodies home, but I refused. I just didn't think I could do that.

We stayed there repairing airplanes until we were shipped out. We had to leave two groups behind because the night before we left, they broke into a liquor store and stole some stuff and beat the man up. One of them was the guy that owed me money, so I never got my money back. I never knew what happened to them. When we shipped out, we were all broke because our pay checks and orders had gone on to Guam. There was one guy who had a little money and he bought me a carton of cigarettes. Our orders had to go on because we were replacing some guys that were coming home and they had to know how many of us there were and what we would be doing. On the way over there, I got caught sleeping in one morning so they had me on guard duty, twelve midnight until eight in the morning. I took two packs of cigarettes out of my carton and hid the rest in my sea bag. That night on guard I was sitting in a wood chair on the fan tail of the ship and the ship listed for some reason and I had the chair leaned against the tool room sitting on two legs. It slid out and rolled to the fan tail of the ship and the rail kept me from falling in the ocean. It scared me to death. I thought they would have left me in the ocean and would wonder what happened to me. I never went to sleep on watch again. When I got back to my quarters, my cigarettes were gone and I made an announcement- "if my cigarettes don't return in a short period, someone is going to be leaving this ship because I will find out who got them". That afternoon, I checked my sea bag, and low and behold, they were there and only one pack was missing.

We went on to Guam. It took sixteen days and nights. We got in seeing distance of Hawaii, the big island, and met a hospital ship. Red Cross was in charge. A guy had died of yellow fever on our ship and they came out to get the body. We didn't know where we were going until we got there. As far as we knew, the war was over and our ship was just taking us over there. We were replacing another unit. Everyone from our unit didn't go to the same place. Some went to other islands. When we reached Guam, we had to go to shore on a landing boat and wade water knee deep part of the way, fully clothed, with our gear on our back. When we got to shore with all our gear, we were assigned a hut, six people to a hut, then they gave us a chow card telling us which chow hall to go to. They gave us a beer card and we could have three beers a day. They had to punch your card and when I got to the beer garden, the guy in charge I had met in California when we were stationed there. He said, "Does that say three cans or three cases?" So he gave me three cases and we had a big party that night.

We were curious to know what was on the other end of the island, so one Sunday we went down there and went to their chow hall to see if they had the same thing we had. It was a B-29 base. Only two of us went, me and my close friend. While we were in chow line, someone slapped me on the back and I was ready to fight, but when I turned around, it was a guy that was raised in the same community back in Texas that I grew up in. We had quite a reunion. We had so many things to talk about.

While we were on Guam, it was not all fun. One afternoon, 16 Japanese soldiers came down from the hills and attacked our chow hall. We didn't have any way to fight back, but we just got behind a concrete wall and some were killed. They went back to the hills. They raided the dumpsters to find food to eat and they would kill animals that belong to the natives there to eat too. One of the Japanese found a Life magazine in the dumpster and found out the war was over. They didn't know the war was over because they had been hiding out so they came down and surrendered and became prisoners of the war. One of the prisoners had gone to school in California and knew our language. When they found that magazine, that's how they found out the war was over. They came down with rifles up with white cloth on them and surrendered. They were confined to a specific area in the camp but they ate as a group in our chow hall. I don't know what the outcome was because we left the island before they did.

We toured the island one day and went into a cave. My buddy found a rifle and a Japanese sword and wrapped them up in a sheet and said, "I'm going to let you have these because I don't think I can get this home". So I brought them home. The gun wouldn't fire, they were just souvenirs. And we had a party before we left the island. I went to get my laundry from this lady who did laundry and she gave me a gallon of Sake, so we all got lit and went to the movies and we got a little loud and they made us leave.

While we were on the island, I was their entertainer. I could sing all of a very popular country singers' songs and they would come and get me to sing at their parties and we had a very good guitar player and he would play and I would sing. I should have pursued that instead of the profession I took.

A while before we left the island, we were playing poker and I bluffed the Chief Petty Officer and won a good pot and he got mad at me. On Sunday before we left we went in to take our showers and someone had put newspaper in the toilet and stopped it up. The Chief Petty Officer told me to clean out the toilet and I said "what with" and he said, "with your hands." I refused and he said, "Are you refusing my orders?" "I said, yes sir, I am." My buddy said, "I'll do it" and I said, "No you won't", and he said, "You want me to get the Officer of the day?" And I said, "Yes". He came in and I told him I refused his orders and the Officer of the day ask the Chief Petty Officer if he would clean it out with his hands and he said, "no, that's not my job." He said, "it's not his either. You get the right tools for the job or you do it." So he said, "you better hope you don't go back on the same ship that I do." He had it in for me over that poker game.

One thing I remember that happened while I was on the island, we were assigned to paint a Quonset Hut and we were on an extension ladder and the paint hose broke loose and was spraying paint every place and I was trying to catch it and I fell and landed on my left hip and it has bothered me ever since. I'm not asking for sympathy, just telling it like it happened. I didn't go to sick bay because we were going to ship out and I didn't want to miss the boat going back to the States.

Heading Home

The morning we left shore in Guam, we had been
out to sea about two hours. We had been anchored side
by side to an ammunition ship and it blew up sometimes.
During that day, our Captain was notified that we were
facing a ninety-foot tidal wave and the Captain ordered to
set sail south for twenty four hours to try to get around it.
By the time it got to us, it was about forty foot. At times
you could reach the water and then you would be forty
foot above the water. The ship was bucking up and down
and we were scared to death. I was thinking about
getting home to my family and wondering if we were

going to drown out there in the ocean with no one around. But it finally calmed down, and we all settled down and the rest of the trip on to California was pretty calm.

When they issued me my chow pass, both hands were full and they stuck it in my shirt pocket and it blew out and I didn't know what I was going to do or what in the world would happen next. But someone told me I could go to an area and they would give me a pass and they did and it was one that I could use at any of the chow halls on the ship and it was one like they give the crew. One night they announced chow hall #......I don't remember the number..... they had to empty one of the reefers (freezer) so they could put a man in it that had passed away until we got to the states. So they gave me five gallons of ripple ice cream and I took it back to my bunk and we had an ice cream party. We were already passed the point of no return so they had to keep him there until we got to the States.

The rest of the trip was pretty pleasant but the weather was awfully warm so most of the time we slept on deck with just our blanket. There was not much to do coming home except exercise so we had an arena set up and we would have boxing matches and the winner would get 2 cartons of cigarettes and the loser would get one. They were only fifty cents a carton but even at that price, sometimes they were hard to buy between paydays. Some of the other guys did the same thing that I did, I made my mother an allotment for twenty dollars a payday and the government matched it. I wanted to know my mother had money she needed to help the family.

But before we left Guam, I had two pair boxing gloves and I soaked them in mineral oil to soften them I thought, but it actually made them hard. We had a job during the week but on the weekend we had to find ways for entertainment so we started matching up to box. This one guy from California heard I was pretty good in the ring, so we got in the ring and he said to just spar, but he caught me looking into the sun and he hit me so hard he nearly locked my jaw. I backed off and I thought to myself, if that's the way you want to play.....so I hit him on the back with a pretty good lick and busted his boil that was on the back of his neck. He turned white and told the guy to take them off (gloves), so I took mine off because I didn't know if I was going to have to run or what, because he had told me before we started that I had better not hit his boil. But he came over and told me I was pretty salty and he went to sick bay and they told him I did them a favor 'cause they didn't have to lance it. But I did get whipped up real bad one time from this little Spanish guy from El Paso. Man, he hit me all over. I didn't want any more of him. He was a lot shorter than me, but he was quick. He was a feather weight champion before he came in the service, but I didn't know that. He was the same guy that bought me a carton of cigarettes going over when someone stole my cigarettes.

We finally got to where we could see the San Francisco shoreline and everyone rushed to the port side of the ship to get a look at land. The Captain came on and said "get off the rail and equalize the weight of the ship if you want to anchor this vessel!" And we did. We got off the ship when we anchored and we headed to the first place we could find to eat and that was my first time to eat pizza. I didn't really like it. I was thinking more like beans and corn bread, but we had a couple of beers with the pizza and then we headed to a base to get a good shower and a good bunk to sleep in. The next day we rode the train to Newton, Kansas for our discharge. We had to be checked out by the Doctor and the Doctor said, "What happened to your eye?" And I said, "It was like that when I came in." He said, "It doesn't say so, if you will stay for 72 hours, you can get a pension." But I didn't want to stay and lie about it because I knew it happened when I tried to dot that "i" in Ohio with my BB gun several years before I went to service. All I wanted to do was get

home to check on my family.

After the Navy

When I got home, my family had moved back to
Glendale and I said no more farming for me. So I went to
my sister's in Pittsburg, Texas where she and her
husband had moved and he was working on cars. He and
I were going to buy old cars and fix them up and sell
them. But it didn't work out and meantime, my family
had moved to Carrollton, Texas. This man from
Carrollton came down to East Texas and moved them to
his place which was a dairy in Carrollton and my sister
younger than me went to work in a café. My dad asked
me to work a couple of days or so and I did, and then I

told him I wasn't going to do that and I went to Dallas to sign up for my unemployment since I was just discharged and had not gotten a real job yet. But they questioned me and I got upset and left. I never got any pay and when I went back to get my car, it had been stolen and I had to walk every step of the way back to Carrollton. The next day someone took me to Dallas and I took a brand new saddle I had bought when I got home from the service and traded it in on a '37 Ford. I didn't need the saddle because my dad had borrowed money on my horse and the bank took the horse along with the other farm animals.......and back to my car that was stolen, they found it all stripped and I didn't have insurance so I had to start over again. Now, since I had my '37 Ford, I could look for work.

Settling Down

I went to work as a carpenter and I beat my fingers all up and cut my thumb real bad, and I decided that wasn't for me. So I went to work in a cabinet shop for sixty cents an hour, and I decided this is not going to get it, so I got the shop approved as a V.A. school. That way I drew ninety dollars a month from the V.A. and they gave me two hundred dollars' worth of tools. In two years, I was to be making $1.25 an hour with my regular raise and while I was schooling and working there I would eat lunch at the café in town where my sister worked. I took my sister to work every day and she would ride home with me when I got off work and we would go places together. My sister was working at the café on the square in Carrollton and she made friends with a girl that worked there after school. They became real good friends and ran around together after work until time to go home. I met this girl and little did I know that a year later she would be my wife. We dated for seven months, and on June 8th, 1947, we got married. We double dated with my sister and her boyfriend and they went to Rockwall with us to get married, and while there, they decided to get married too!

We rented a cute little house that this lady had built on her father's place and we lived there two months before I finished my 2 years of schooling. The man that owned the shop sold it and I went to work in a shop in Farmers Branch for the second year. But after I finished school, he didn't want to pay me $1.25 an hour because I would be making more than the other guys. So I went to work in a shop in Letot for $1.25 an hour, and after I got off, I would work for the shop in Farmers Branch. I was working two jobs. So I bought this house, a new house, on my G.I. Bill. It was a cute little house with hardwood floors, 2 bedrooms, living room, bath, and large kitchen. We loved it and it only cost $4950 and the payment was $39.00 a month for twenty years. And then we found out my wife was pregnant, and we were thrilled but she was very sick for the first three months. On April Fool's Day the next year, we had our first child, a 9lb, 12oz baby boy with black hair, blue eyes. Everyone loved him and he loved everyone, never saw a stranger, and still doesn't today.

We lived in our house in Farmers Branch for four years and we sold it and bought a new house in Carrollton, a larger house in a new addition. It was $8500 and our payments were $59.00 a month. My wife's great aunt kept our son and my wife went to work and things were good. Then when our son was four, my wife found out she was pregnant again. So in 1952, we had a daughter. She weighed less than six pounds. She was so little and cute, lots of black hair and brown eyes. The first night she was home she was crying and our son said, "I didn't want a girl 'cause they cry too much." But, he got over that real quick and he loved her to death and still does.

Sad Times

But 1952 was a very sad time too. Before our daughter was born, I lost my mother to lung cancer and that was a very sad time in my life and also a sad time for my sisters and brothers. She left behind a son 16 years old and one 14, and a daughter 12 years old, and it was a sad time for the whole family. She was always the back bone that kept the family together and she was so worried about them knowing how my dad was. But we all helped out with them and they lived a time with each of us, which is myself and one of my sisters. Dad went on doing his thing with a bottle when he could get it. I bought a plot in the Farmers Branch cemetery and it had

5 spaces, so we buried mom there. Then, a year and a half

later, the 16 year old was playing with a gun while

visiting one of my married brothers and his wife, and he

accidently shot himself. We buried him by our mother

and that was another very sad time of our lives. He was

such a handsome young boy and to die at such an early

time of his life. We all missed him. He was a good kid and

a hard worker, and it was very hard for my brother who

saw it happen.

Watch Out!

Before we bought the house in Carrollton, I told my wife about it and she was so scared about that much money and I told her not to worry, it would be ok, and sure enough it was. One night, we went to see my older sister who lived in Garland and we had a new '52 Chevrolet. We were coming home on Belt Line Rd. in Addison and there was a train across the tracks. I wasn't showing any signs of stopping and my wife said, "Are you going to hit that train?" I hit the brake and did a quick turn on to Addison Rd. I was looking over the train at the light on the power plant in Coppell and that scared me to death having my wife and babies in the car and what

could have happened because I would have hit that train

if my wife had not got my attention!

The Entrepreneur and Craftsman

In 1954, I wanted to go to work for myself, so I traded our home in Carrollton for a house and a 30X40 ft. shop building with all the cabinet shop equipment in it on a half-acre. It was a real nice place and I got plenty of work. I did work for several builders and I got other work too.

My wife's mom had given her a wash pot that had holes in the bottom that she used to plant flowers in and I took it to a friends' blacksmith shop and asked him if he could make me a grill out of it. He put legs on it and a tray on the side of it, and took a truck rim off a one-ton truck and put a stake on it and mounted it on top and made a lid. We would have company and cook hamburgers on it in the back yard. It was great. We used it for years and then our son used it for years after he married, and now our grandson is still using it after 60 years. He has other grills but he said that was the best one. We all cooked steaks on it too and it also had a lift out grill so we could put charcoal in it.

I built the counter in the first restaurant in the terminal building at the Addison airport. I did work in about every business in Carrollton as well as the schools and churches. While we lived there, my wife started to Beauty school and we only had one car so I had to take the kids to the sitters and my wife to school and pick them up in the evening. I would work late in the shop some nights and after my wife finished school, I put her in a Beauty Shop in Carrollton and built all the fixtures. Then I bought a truck off one of my builders and my wife could go to work and take the kids to the sitter and I could do my work at a different pace. Some guys kept speeding in front of our house and I reported them and they got mad and put sugar in my gas tank and my truck wouldn't run. A neighbor traded his truck in and I went to the town dealership and bought it. I traded in my wife's '52 Chevrolet and got a '55 Chevrolet. We thought we had to have that '55 and then when my little brother got out of the service, I bought the '52 back for him and he drove it for a couple of years.

My wife got tired of all the hours she had to work at the beauty shop and she needed more set hours with our son in school. I sold the shop to one of my wife's instructors that she had in beauty school and my wife went to work at Texas Instrument in 1957. A good opportunity came to me to go to work at the airline. While working at the airline center, I still did work for the public and I contracted a job from the airline to build ticket counter inserts to be shipped to Utah. I also built a whole kitchen and shipped it by truck to Corpus Christi,

Texas. While I still had my shop in Addison, I designed a child's desk for my daughter, which in later years I would get a patent on, and I also built a hutch for my wife. She used it for years and then my sister used it and her daughter is still using it today.

Do-si-do

While my wife was working at T.I., one day she came home and told me they were getting a square dance club started and asked me if I would like to take lessons. I said, "No", that's silly, I don't care for that. And then I felt bad because she really wanted too, so I told her the next day to sign us up and we started and we both loved it. We had so much fun. We belonged to three clubs and danced three nights a week. We really got to be good and other people from town would come and watch us. We took the kids with us and they loved to watch us and later when they were older, they both started dancing too.

Raising Cattle

Then in 1961, we wanted to raise cattle, so we bought a place in East Texas and bought some cows and built a shop building on the place. We had a big house and barn and we leased more land so we had grass for the cows, but we had a drought and had to buy hay and haul water for the cows. So two years of that and we sold our cows and came back to Carrollton. I went back to the airline and got my seniority back and my wife went back to T.I and got her seniority. While we were in East Texas, I bid on 23 kitchens and built 22 of them. I did work in the bank building and some of the other businesses in town. I just couldn't get away from the woodwork.

Why the Story Almost Wasn't Told

We bought this house in Carrollton and it was a real good location for our kids to go to school. Our son graduated from high school and our daughter finished Jr. High and then she graduated from high school. We bought her a new Camaro and we told her we were going to take her on a vacation. It would be our last vacation with her before she married and we were going to see the blue grass of Kentucky. We went in the Camaro and it rained all week. I kept telling her I was going to get some of those big tobacco leaves but it wouldn't stop raining and it was too muddy to get in the fields. One afternoon we were sightseeing and it had been raining real hard. I was driving pretty fast and we rounded this curve and the water was already over the banks and out over the bridge that crossed the river and all I could do was step on the gas, say "God be with us", and we just planed that water. When we got to the other side, we met the truck that was coming to put up barricades to close the road. I was so nervous I had to get out of the car and walk around awhile. The man with the barricades asked me if I crossed the river. I told him, "yes, just now". He said, "well, you must have planed that river to have made it across without drowning." A couple of miles down the road was a Holiday Inn and we stopped and got a room and we all three got in bed with our clothes on to get warm and settle down. A couple hours later, we got up, showered and dressed, and went down to eat dinner. That was a close call that we did not soon forget.

The next morning when we went to check out, the fire truck and ambulance was there, this little boy had gotten into his mother's purse and taken some of her medication and they had to pump his stomach. So that was not a very fun vacation and our daughter slept in the back seat most of the way home.

Our Children- Teenage Memories

Both our children were members of the Rodeo Club. While in high school, our son worked after school for a local grocery store and ambulance service so he had some experiences that he would remember forever. While our daughter was in school, she was a candy striper at the local hospital.

Western Stores and Wasps

I put in a Western store with a partner and between us all working, my wife and his wife, we kept our jobs at the airlines and T.I. and I would still get calls to do wood work. A guy that built saddles used a building I had next to the western store to build our saddles for the store and he built one for our daughter. It was beautiful. One morning he came in the store and asked me if I had a match and I asked him what he needed it for. He had some cloth on a long pole and he said he wanted to burn a wasp nest. I said no, you might burn the building down, just let them settle down and I'll take care of it. I just reached up and pinched it off and threw the nest down. He couldn't believe it. I said, "If you're not scared of them, they're not scared of you." I do that all the time.

But in 1973, we sold our part of the western store to my sister and we moved back to East Texas and bought another place and built another western store. Our son had gotten married after he graduated and our daughter got married in 1972 and moved to Fort Polk, Louisiana, where her husband was stationed in the service. So we built the western store and it was a very good location. We got business from four states- Texas, Oklahoma, Louisiana, and Arkansas. We had a good business and things were fine except for my wife. She was not happy there. She missed being in Carrollton and worried about her mom and the kids being gone and she was brooding around. I asked her what was wrong and she said, "I want to go back home to Carrollton, but I know we can't." I said, "If you're not happy, I'll just sell this place and we'll go back."

Return to Carrollton and Woodwork

We had a big sale and in no time we were back in Carrollton. Later, we sold the store building and a little house on the same property and the big house we bought to live in. Our daughter had a baby boy and her husband was not acting like a husband and father should. He ran off and left them. He didn't want to work, he was not a provider, so she moved back to Carrollton with us and we bought a nice home in north Carrollton. Then a friend of ours who was in real estate told us about this place she had in Carrollton that was close to half an acre with a nice house on it and it was zoned so we could build a shop building. So we bought it and built a little house and a

30x40 shop building for a cabinet shop and my in-laws lived in the little house.

I did work for the schools and cabinets for builders and I started building the child's desk that I had a patent on. We sold a lot of desks to a well-known furniture store in Dallas and it was featured in the newspaper. We got a lot of orders and we shipped them to a lot of different baby stores. At the same time, I worked for an airplane refurbishing company building interiors and refurbishing corporate jets for private companies. I did all the woodwork. Arco Gas and Oil Co said when I finished their plane that it was the prettiest one they had ever been in. I also did one for Greyhound Bus Line and one for Prudential Insurance Co. They each turned out real nice. Then I went to work for another company that did the same thing. I did work in the Starbucks (®) plane. I also did the interior for a C130 for a foreign country. I trimmed out the door going into the cockpit. It was teak wood. I made the molding on a table saw and when they got the plane back home, the President wanted 100 feet of that molding to frame pictures. I don't know if it was for his home or office. After that airplane, I semi-retired, but the city of Addison called me to build a witness stand for their new courthouse and they wanted it built in a way that it could be used on the right or left side of the Judge.

Raising Emu

We lived there for 17 years and the property joined the school property. They wanted to expand so we sold to the school and a friend of ours had just gone into the emu business and that was supposed to grow into something big, so we bought some emus. For a while we kept them on a place in Carrollton and then we decided we needed to find some acreage, so I found this place in Cook County with ten acres. It was a beautiful place with a real nice house, tool house, and a barn and it had a pool with large catfish. I built houses and pens for the emu birds and we all loved the place. We got it all fixed up the way we wanted it and I had not been doing very well. I had diabetes and I couldn't get it regulated and the kids had to come up on the weekends and mow and help with the birds. We had a storm one night and it blew some of the houses over and the fence and about that time the bottom fell out of the emu sales. The market didn't work out for emu meat either, so we decided we needed to sell the birds and the kids said, "Y'all need to come back close to us and the doctors so we can help you get well." So we had no problem selling the place. It was beautiful and my wife loved it and all the big oak trees.

Found Something to Do

So we came back and bought a house in Lewisville where our daughter and son-in-law lived and in about a year, I got my diabetes under control with the doctor's help and my family. I decided one day I wanted to find something to do, so I went to Sam's store and they hired me and I came home and told my wife I had gotten a job at Sam's, and if she wanted to work, she probably could get one too. Four days later, she went to work at Sam's. I started out in the bakery and did a good job, but later went to the door as a door greeter. My wife went to work in the pizza café until they got the jewelry set up and then she went to the jewelry department. We ended up working twelve years and loved every minute of it. We met so many nice people and became close friends with some of them and some of the people we worked with are still there and we love visiting with them.

While I was there in 2006, I had lung cancer and had surgery and about a year later, I fell and broke my neck. In 2010, I had a stroke and at the hospital, I had a second stroke and my wife started having some heart problems. So in 2012, we had to retire. My sister came and helped us out for a while but her health was not too good either. Our daughter and son-in-law moved in with us to help us, but they both worked and it was hard on them.

Sharing Life and Memories

So, we sold our house and moved to Pinewood Hills and we have been here going on three years. We had to sell the car because we did not feel safe driving anymore. I guess that was one of the hardest things we had to do. We still miss our car, but Pinewood Hills has a bus and a very helpful driver that takes us to the doctor or shopping on Tuesday and Thursday when needed. We have entertainers that come in and sing, some play the guitar or piano, and some use a karaoke machine. They have Bingo twice a week and they have card games or dominoes and other games for people our age if you want to participate. If you are not able to do the games, you can always sit on the porch and rock and visit with others that like to just sit on the porch and rock and talk about their kids, grandkids, great grandkids, or what they did or where they came from in their life time- some very interesting stories. There are people from all states. They are here because this is where their kids are or some of their kid's jobs brought them in this area. Our kids live close by and if we need them, they are here. They are very good about helping us and seeing that we have the things we need, and they check on us daily. We are blessed with nine wonderful grandchildren who we love dearly and see as often as possible. We also have the special blessing of many great-grandchildren and also great-great-grandchildren too numerous to count! We truly are blessed!

We have a lot of friends and it's like one big family. We have seen a lot of people come and go and you get close to some and it's hard to see them go. We talk to each other about our childhood days and how hard it was.

Most of them had about the same kind of life I did as a

child because people used to have large families and

growing up they had to help with the farming like I did.

But not all were treated the way me and my siblings were.

They came first not the booze. I just wish my mother

could have been with us longer and we could have given

her a better life. I only had one brother, my oldest, that

kind of took the road my dad took. He liked to drink and

it cost him his family. He was good at woodwork and

construction, but he couldn't leave the bottle alone and he

died way too young. I had thirteen brothers and sisters

and two died at 2 and 3 years old with the flu and one

was stillborn. I loved them all and was especially close to

my 2 sisters just younger than me. When I started

driving, I would take them places and we worked the

fields together. They really hated for me to go to the Navy

and I hated to leave them too. But I hated to leave my

mother the worst. After my mother passed away, I

helped the younger ones and had a lot of fun with them. Life was a lot different for them. They didn't have to move from farm to farm trying to raise a crop. I know mom would have been so proud of all of us, the men and women we became, and that we all had professions and treated our kids and spouses with love and respect like she instilled in us. It's been a hard row to hoe, but I sure am glad I did.

My dad and mom

My parents on the farm

Cotton field work just had to get done!

My Mom and some of my brothers and sisters

Heading to school

Navy days

Me and my wife in the early days

Our young family

On vacation- pictured with my brother-in-law

Me and my bride- one of my favorite pictures

Our midlife years

Some of my creations:

Ironing board cabinet

One of several desks I made, still used today as a vanity

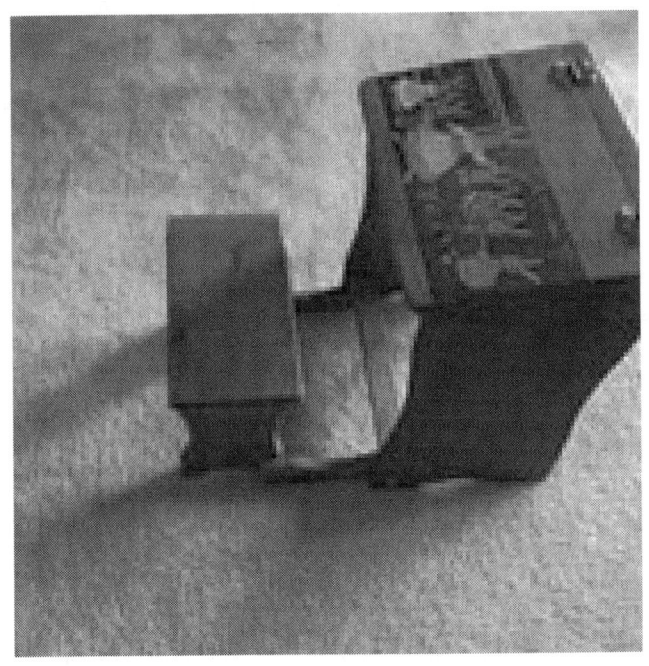

The child's desk I created and is patented

Me and my bride today, in our golden years

90 years old, a new author, and thinking of my next project......

24900412R00091

Made in the USA
San Bernardino, CA
11 October 2015